D1053684

EAT YOUR DRINK

EAT YOUR DRINK

·· CULINARY COCKTAILS ··

MATTHEW BIANCANIELLO

PHOTOGRAPHS BY MIA WASILEVICH

DEY ST.

AN IMPRINT OF
WILLIAM MORROW *PUBLISHERS*

EAT YOUR DRINK. Copyright © 2016 by Matthew Biancaniello.
All rights reserved. Printed in the United States of America. No part
of this book may be used or reproduced in any manner whatsoever
without written permission except in the case of brief quotations
embodied in critical articles and reviews. For information address
HarperCollins Publishers, 195 Broadway, New York, NY 10007.

HarperCollins books may be purchased for educational, business,
or sales promotional use. For information please e-mail the
Special Markets Department at SPsales@harpercollins.com.

FIRST EDITION

Designed by Ashley Tucker

Library of Congress Cataloging-in-Publication Data has been applied for.

ISBN 978-0-06-239128-5

16 17 18 19 20   OV/RRD   10 9 8 7 6 5 4 3 2 1

For my amazing partner and love of my life, Quincy Mary Johns Coleman, and my twin boys, Kai Nash and Coleman Buddy. You are the only things in my life that are not an illusion. I love you with all my heart.

CONTENTS

MAIN COURSE 69

DESSERT 97

AFTER DINNER 112

ACKNOWLEDGMENTS

––––––– //// –––––––

Special thanks to Mia Wasilevich, for her amazing photography, guidance, and creative spirit.

Luke Fisher, for being my rock and taking me to the next level, you kill it every time. I love you, brother.

And thank you to all the people who have supported me, made me better and braver, and lifted me up to higher ground. I love you all.

Bradley Tuck

Pascal Baudar

Andrew Oliveri

Geri and Steven Miller of the Cook's Garden by HGEL

Bill and Barbara Spencer of Windrose Farm

Romeo and everyone at Coleman Farms

Laura from J.J.'s Lone Daughter Ranch

Laura Avery

Lance from CapRock Gin and Jack Rabbit Hill Farm

Nicholas Family Farms

Dirk from LA FungHi

Mud Creek Farms

David Ravandi from 123 Tequila

Charlotte Voisey and Hendrick's Gin

Bryan Chenault

David Othenin-Girard and K&L Wine Merchants

Michel Dozois and Névé Ice

Lauren and Marissa from Bar and Garden

Joe Keeper

Dragos Axinte and Novo Fogo

Don Jacinto

Greg Debolt

Brian Hepp and Hepp's Salt Co.

Kat Odell

Betty Hallock

Lenny from Gourmet Blends

Jason Park of Maru

Marcus Fan

David Greenberg

David Farkas

Kurt Charron and Chareau

Gaston Martinez

Jenn Harris

Caroline Pardilla

David Farkas

Carlito Jocson

Harald Hermann

Vasiliki Biancaniello, for giving me your sense of style

The Fat Dog

Anthony Biancaniello, for taking me to Wilson Farm every Sunday

Mark Biancaniello, for instilling in me a love for nature and bees

Jean Hale Coleman

Dabney Coleman

Julia Cheiffetz

HarperCollins and Dey Street Books

P.J. Pesce

Vikki Karan

Erin Malone

Matthew Kang

Julie Wolfson

Josh Lurie

Shane Liem

Perry Kalmus

Tatsu Oiye

Lesley Suter

Casey Kramer

Bryson Igarta

Melissa's Produce

And to all the amazing guests I have served over the years!

FOREWORD

———————— //// ————————

It was a random midsummer Sunday in 2011. A friend and I were driving around LA looking to have a great cocktail. Reaching for my phone, I searched for "Creative Cocktails," and the Library Bar in the Roosevelt Hotel popped up. My friend said, "Okay, let's go to Hollywood." Walking through the labyrinth of dark corridors of the hotel, we found the small bar. There, at the forefront, stood a man behind a towering fence of herbs, jars of mysterious infusions, and just-picked fresh fruit. I knew I had stumbled into the right place. After five minutes of conversation with Matthew Biancaniello, the universe had already begun intertwining us with threads of creativity and familiarity. I quickly realized that this gentleman thought about his craft exactly the way I approach my cuisine. He was passionate, and his enthusiasm left a spark of inspiration on the palates of everyone who was fortunate enough to taste one of his creations. I then became graced. Cocktail number one came in a tall glass with a rooftop of edible flowers. Cocktail number two came in a short whiskey glass with layered textures; I was blown away. Not only that, he left me in a state of bewilderment. In my mind, I had at this point coined him a "liquid chef." Never before had I experienced flavors and textures in a cocktail like I did with Matthew. Then, before I knew it, hours had flown by and we had stayed longer than expected. Upon saying our good-byes, we said we would keep in touch.

A year or so later, I reached out to Matthew and asked him if he would be interested in collaborating in a cocktail pairing to one of my conceptual/design-inspired dinners. Who am I? I'm a chef with a dining group called CR8 (pronounced "create"). I started my career as a private chef to Hollywood celebrities such as Eddie Murphy and Antonio Banderas, as well as business moguls such as Paul Allen. I collected my training by attending five schools in France. At one point, deciding to add pastry chef to my roster, I attended the prestigious Chocovic chocolate school in Barcelona.

My dinners are all connected with designers (industrial, interior, cutlery, glass, furniture, etc.). I first create a master concept. This acts as a thematic roof under which are the microconcepts. These become courses of dishes shown and expressed with the functional direction that the designers have created. The CR8 I wanted Matthew to be a part of was called "The Art Of," the concept of which was a direct focus on the artistry of uncommon topics and elements. He was more than excited to collaborate with me. Meeting after meeting with Matthew, the ideas and flavor combinations became more and more explosive. I knew he was going to catapult this experience to a new level.

Matthew is a self-taught mixologist with a natural gift of endless creativity and mastery of degustation. The synergy that exists between Matthew and me is neutral and symphonic. We finish each other's ideas, not with words, but with ingredients and tastes that spark new inner directions within us. This is culinary poetry in pure form.

In early 2015, I was blessed once again with another collaboration with Matthew in Seattle, at my "Liquid Forms" CR8 event. There was a new maturity in both of us that was noticeable, and with that, another level of creativity we had both reached. His creations were brilliant and subsequently took my conceptual dishes to a sublime realm.

In a world of endless cookbooks in many styles and cuisines, this book marks the beginning of a recipe collection all its own. His wizardry is apparent, as he lays out this edible novel as a savory or sweet chef might course through a fine-dining event. The title of the book gains meaning as you notice the unorthodox incorporation of edible ingredients such as sea urchin (uni), arugula, beets, and oysters. Starting with Amuse-Bouche, small drinks and bites explode with tastes twice their size. The liquid bites continue into First Course and Second Course, where you will discover a beet horseradish and cucumber cocktail oozing sexiness. The Main Course hits high notes with a fifteen-ingredient Bloody Mary, which is every bit as delicious as the steps it takes to create it. Like that accomplished feeling of making our very first stock or pâté, these steps become a labor of love, but only if you choose this mission.

The ideas flourish further as the Dessert chapter grabs your attention with White Truffle Eggnog served in a real emu egg!

While you read this book, one thing is certain: it will start to expand your own creativity in ways you never expected. How is this possible? In chapter after chapter, you will notice that flavors and ingredients are not bound to any predetermined rules. You will start to question your own boundaries, see new possibilities, and realize that Matthew has just unlocked a side of you that you didn't even know was there.

ROBERTO CORTEZ,
CR8 Dining Experimental
Seattle, Washington

INTRODUCTION

////

I never would have gotten the job at the Hollywood Roosevelt Hotel in July 2008 if I hadn't known the bar manager, Tiffany Russo, through yoga. The Roosevelt had gone through a thirty-million-dollar renovation and it was one of the hottest places in Los Angeles. She decided to give me a chance, but because I barely had any experience, she put me in a smaller and quieter bar called the Library Bar. The Library Bar was a thirty-five-seat bar that was mostly used for the overflow of young club kids slurping up vodka Red Bulls on Friday and Saturday nights. On all the other nights, it was a ghost town. On my first night behind the stick, someone asked me for a Cosmopolitan and I had to duck down and whisper to the bartender next to me, "What's in a Cosmopolitan?" That's how little I knew about bartending.

The whole craft cocktail movement was just beginning in LA, and there was no one I could turn to in the hotel for guidance. As a matter of fact, I didn't know much back then, but I did know that something was wrong when a classic cocktail on the menu, a Martinez, was made with maraschino cherry juice instead of maraschino cherry liqueur.

Hotel bars are notorious for being overpriced, and the Library Bar was no exception. The drinks on the cocktail menu were $15 and I instinctively knew they weren't worth that much at the time. So the first thing I decided to do was to start to swap out the existing ingredients with fresh ones from the local farmers' markets.

I am half Greek and half Italian, and when I was growing up, my Greek grandparents grew a lot of vegetables in their own garden. During high school, I went to Wilson Farm in Lexington, Massachusetts, with my father every Sunday to stock up on fresh fruits and vegetables for the week. So it seemed like a natural thing for me to go out and find as many local ingredients as I could.

After a few weeks of going to the farmers' market in Santa Monica on Wednesdays, which in my opinion is the greatest market in the world, my manager stopped by to see how I was doing. She tried one of my drinks and couldn't believe the flavors and freshness of the cocktail. I told her that it had fresh pomegranate juice in it, and she was blown away that I was just buying all of these fresh ingredients with my own money. She offered to give me a hundred dollars a week so I could continue my weekly addiction, but I ended up spending four hundred dollars a week on things that I had never seen or heard of in my life. That first year, I spent eight thousand dollars out of my own pocket educating myself on herbs, ice, and as many different alcohols as possible.

A combination of things make going to the farmers' market so extraordinary. A lot of the produce is organic, and most of it was picked either the day before or that morning, so it is at its maximum peak of flavor. But what probably makes the market the most extraordinary is the diversity of the farmers' nationalities. From Mexican to French, from Filipino to Brazilian, these farmers end up growing things that are not only indigenous to their native lands but that they are also nostalgic for. I've been shopping there for more than seven years, and I am constantly amazed at all the new things I keep seeing from season to season. Just when I think I know everything, something new and magical will pop up in a completely different form. I feel like I am in the farmers' market mafia where farmers like J.J.'s Lone Daughter would set aside things like strawberry figs for me before putting them out on the stand.

After a year and a half of creating the concept of farm to glass for the Library Bar at the Hollywood Roosevelt Hotel, I realized that there was something more profound going on than just making cocktails.

I quickly understood that I had four impressions to make on the imbiber. First was the name, second was the look, third was the smell, and fourth was the taste. And over the last seven years it has become my passion to tell a story with each libation traveling across that bar with the hopes of transporting someone to another place.

I grew up with an alcoholic mother, and alcohol became a very negative and painful experience for me. I associated it with the ultimate path of destruction, and being behind a bar was the last place I thought I'd find myself. So, a year and a half into mixing cocktails and witnessing the effect I was having on the guests, I understood that I was slowly, one drink at a time, rescripting my relationship with alcohol. Making it something that was beautiful, fresh, and needing to be savored. And through this repetition, I unintentionally was able to heal my wounds, freeing myself to dive even deeper into my craft.

My favorite thing to hear from customers is not that this is the best drink they have ever had but that they have never had anything like it before. I hope that this book can shatter this myth of mixology a little bit. A lot of my work can look intimidating for the home bartender to do, but my drinks actually follow a simple formula, and the true art and passion come from the individual's choice of ingredients.

There are so many amazing books out there on the craft of bartending, bar techniques, and beautifully reimagined classic cocktails that are great references and foundations for your work. This book is intended to complement those works and open up your eyes to what's possible, to encourage you to explore what is local, native, and extraordinary about where you live and how you can incorporate it.

My mission is to be constantly creating, finding unusual fruits and herbs that I can store in the memory banks of the cocktail enthusiast forever. It is a passion that is reignited every time I stroll the farmers' market or encounter a guest for the first time. I am very lucky to be around the greatest markets in the world, which consistently surprise me with each season and allow me to stretch my imagination in ways I didn't even think were possible. I hope this book inspires you as much as writing it has inspired me.

AMUSE-BOUCHE

––––––––– //// –––––––––

Amuse-bouche literally means "fun in your mouth" or "a laugh in the mouth." This is something that is usually given on the house to diners at the beginning of a meal. It's meant to open up their palates and ignite what is about to come.

A couple of years into my stint at the Library Bar, I really started to adopt this ritual. I had time to create simple alcoholic bites, or sips. These have developed over the years to incorporate many flavors and textures, but mostly they surprise the guests and deepen their experience.

––––––––– //// –––––––––

One of the most beautiful things you can make is a dehydrated orange or blood orange slice. All the incredible details come out when orange slices are dried, and, when you use a blood orange, they look like stained-glass windows. After years of using dehydrated slices as breathtaking garnishes, I started using them as crackers with goat cheese. • **MAKES 1**

BLOOD ORANGE CHEESE AND CRACKER

\\\\\

1 TABLESPOON SOFT **GOAT CHEESE**, AT ROOM TEMPERATURE

1 **BLOOD ORANGE CRACKER** (RECIPE FOLLOWS)

2 TABLESPOONS **FIG-BOURBON JELLY** (RECIPE FOLLOWS)

5 **LAVENDER BUDS**, FOR GARNISH

\\\\\

Spread the goat cheese on top of the blood orange cracker. Top with the fig-bourbon jelly and garnish with the lavender buds.

BLOOD ORANGE CRACKERS

MAKES 6 TO 8 CRACKERS

Using a bread knife, cut a **blood orange** crosswise into $\frac{1}{16}$-inch-thick slices and dehydrate the slices in a NESCO dehydrator (see Sources, page 153) for 8 hours. Store the blood orange crackers in a plastic freezer bag at room temperature.

FIG-BOURBON JELLY

MAKES 1½ CUPS

2 PINTS SOFT **MISSION FIGS**, HALVED

1 (750-ML) BOTTLE **BASIL HAYDEN'S BOURBON**

Place the figs in an airtight container. Pour the bourbon over the figs and refrigerate for 2 weeks or until the bourbon starts to thicken into a jelly at the bottom of the container. It will keep in the refrigerator for up to 6 months.

Pineapple guavas are nothing like regular guavas. They have a very tart and flowery flavor that is unlike anything I've tasted before. Because they tend to be more on the firm side, I love grilling them to soften and bring out the flavor even more. • **MAKES 4**

GRILLED PINEAPPLE GUAVA

\\\\\

1 **PINEAPPLE GUAVA**, CUT CROSSWISE INTO FOUR ¼-INCH-THICK SLICES

2 OUNCES **123 ORGANIC BLANCO (UNO) TEQUILA**

20 FRESH **THAI BASIL BLOSSOMS**

\\\\\

Heat a grill to high heat (425°F). Grill the pineapple guava slices for 2 minutes on each side. Place each grilled slice on a wide spoon and pour ½ ounce of the tequila on top. Garnish each with 5 basil blossoms.

Finger limes are indigenous to Australia, and Shanley Farms in the Central Coast of California started growing them successfully here about six years ago. The flesh of this amazing citrus fruit can be scooped out and used as a natural lime caviar that works perfectly for an amuse-bouche. • **MAKES 4**

FINGER LIME CAIPIRINHA

////

¾ OUNCE **AGAVE SYRUP** (SEE PAGE 32)

2 OUNCES **NOVO FOGO SILVER CACHAÇA**

2 **FINGER LIMES**

////

In a bowl, mix the agave and cachaça. Halve the limes crosswise and squeeze the lime caviar into the bowl. Let soak for 30 minutes, then spoon the lime caviar back into the lime halves. Alternatively, using a syringe, drip some of the cachaça mixture over the cut ends of the finger lime halves.

Squeeze the lime caviar directly into your mouth—it will be like an instant caipirinha.

Passion fruit is my favorite fruit in the world. When I started my own garden, I planted a small vine in the beginning of the plot. After six months, I got rid of everything else and was looking at a 30-foot vine. I planted the vine with the love of my life on Valentine's Day, not realizing she was pregnant with our twin boys. And as her belly grew, the vine grew. Passion fruit is one of the few things that I buy year-round, even when it's not in season. The flower is outstanding, and its resemblance to the cross is where it gets its name. • **MAKES 1**

PASSION FRUIT CUP

1 FRESH **PASSION FRUIT**

½ OUNCE **CAPPELLETTI VINO APERITIVO AMERICANO ROSSO**

4 DROPS **CURRY LEAF OIL** (SEE OPPOSITE)

Cut the passion fruit in half and rest the bottom half on a shot glass. Pour in the Cappelletti and the curry leaf oil. Grab a spoon and enjoy.

CURRY LEAF OIL

Technique adapted from Chef John Gladdish.

MAKES ABOUT 2 CUPS

1 CUP **CURRY LEAVES**

2 CUPS **NEUTRAL OIL**, SUCH AS GRAPESEED OIL

Bring a pot of water to a boil. Fill a large bowl with ice and water. Blanch the curry leaves in the boiling water for 30 seconds and then shock them in the ice water bath. Drain and squeeze dry with your hands. Place the leaves and oil in a Vitamix or other high-speed blender and puree to make a paste. Transfer to a shallow sauté pan and cook for 5 minutes over medium heat, until the oil turns bright green. Strain the oil through a coffee filter into a storage container. The oil will keep in the refrigerator

There are hundreds of kinds of cherry tomatoes, wonderful for muddling and pickling, but equally great for their firm and delicate texture. Just the stems alone are a work of art. They also make for an opening sensation. They are the perfect bite-size treat, with lots of flavor and juice. The epitome of summer, cherry tomatoes, especially Sungolds, are the easiest to grow and most prolific tomatoes. • **MAKES 6**

STUFFED CHERRY TOMATO

\\\\\

6 **CHERRY TOMATOES,** STEMS INTACT

5 OUNCES **CARAMEL SAUCE** (RECIPE FOLLOWS)

HIMALAYAN PINK SALT SLAB
(OPTIONAL; SEE SOURCES, PAGE 153)

6 OUNCES **APRICOT-INFUSED TEQUILA** (RECIPE FOLLOWS)

\\\\\

Dip the base of each cherry tomato in the caramel sauce. Place them on a Himalayan salt slab, if desired, and let sit for a few minutes. Using a culinary syringe, inject each cherry tomato with 1 ounce of the tequila. Pop them in your mouth.

CARAMEL SAUCE

Technique adapted from Chef Jason Park.
The lemon juice is included to prevent lumping.

MAKES 4 QUARTS

4½ POUNDS **SUGAR**

2 OUNCES FRESH **LEMON JUICE**

2 QUARTS **HEAVY CREAM**, AT ROOM TEMPERATURE

5 OUNCES **UNSALTED BUTTER**, CUT INTO PIECES

Combine the sugar, lemon juice, and 2 cups water in a heavy saucepan and bring to a boil over high heat. Attach a candy thermometer to the side of the pan and boil until the mixture reaches 320°F and caramelizes to a dark golden brown.

Remove from the heat to a cool surface and add the cream. Be careful of splattering. Whisk to combine.

Add the butter and whisk to combine.

Strain and let cool to room temperature. The caramel can be stored in an airtight container in the refrigerator for up to 1 month.

APRICOT-INFUSED TEQUILA

MAKES 1 (750-ML) BOTTLE

---

8 TO 10 **APRICOTS**, PREFERABLY BLENHEIMS,
HALVED AND PITTED

1 (750-ML) BOTTLE **123 ORGANIC BLANCO (UNO) TEQUILA**

Place the apricots in a quart-size jar and pour in
the tequila. Cover and set aside in a cool, dark
place to infuse for 2 weeks. Strain the tequila back
into the bottle. It will keep in the refrigerator for up
to 6 months.

A Moroccan chef taught me the easiest way to get the seeds out of a pomegranate: cut the pomegranate in half, turn one of the halves over a bowl, beat the back of the pomegranate with a spoon, and just watch the voluptuous seeds start dropping like flies. Repeat with the other half and with as many pomegranates as you need. • **MAKES 1**

POMEGRANATE SEEDS

1 CUP FRESH **POMEGRANATE SEEDS**

3 OUNCES **VANILLA-INFUSED CALISAYA** (SEE OPPOSITE)

Place the pomegranate seeds in a bowl, then pour the vanilla-infused Calisaya into the bowl, covering the seeds completely. Let them soak for about 2 hours.

Fill a small hurricane glass with the soaked pomegranate seeds and top with vanilla-infused Calisaya.

VANILLA-INFUSED CALISAYA

Calisaya is a natural and herbal liqueur from Italy with an amazing clean flavor. It is an amaro similar to Campari but doesn't have high-fructose corn syrup or artificial dyes.

MAKES 1 (750-ML) BOTTLE

2 **VANILLA BEANS** (PREFERABLY FROM VANILLA FROM TAHITI; SEE SOURCES, PAGE 153)

1 (750-ML) BOTTLE **CALISAYA**

Split the vanilla beans lengthwise and put them in the bottle of Calisaya. Set aside to infuse for 4 weeks, then it's ready to go—no need to strain or discard the vanilla beans.

We are lucky to have many grapefruit varieties in California. The Oroblanco is the pot of gold of the citrus family because of its sweet and gentle flavor. • **MAKES 2**

OROBLANCO BOWL

\\\\\

1 **RUBY RED GRAPEFRUIT**, HALVED

1 **MORO BLOOD ORANGE**

1 **SATSUMA MANDARIN**

1 **OROBLANCO GRAPEFRUIT**

2 OUNCES **ST. ELIZABETH ALLSPICE DRAM**

2 TABLESPOONS **OLIVE OIL**

8 FRESH **MINT LEAVES**

6 **ARUGULA BLOSSOMS**

\\\\\

Hollow out the Ruby Red grapefruit halves. Peel the membrane from three segments each of the blood orange, mandarin, and Oroblanco grapefruit and cut them into pieces. Place them in a bowl, pour in the allspice dram and the olive oil, and mix.

Stack the mint leaves, roll them up, and cut them crosswise into chiffonade. Add the mint and the whole arugula blossoms to the bowl with the citrus and mix. Refrigerate for 2 hours, then transfer into the hollowed-out grapefruit halves and serve with a spoon.

When I was working with Top Chef Marcel Vigeron on a paired dinner, he told me that the flavors of elderflower and rhubarb went well together, so I decided to make that combination work in an infusion. The bitterness of the rhubarb balances out the sweetness of the St-Germain. • **MAKES 1**

ELDERFLOWER TARTE

4 OUNCES FRESH **MEYER LEMON JUICE**

1 TABLESPOON **TEXTURAS SUCRO**
(SUCROSE ESTERS; SEE SOURCES, PAGE 153)

3 OUNCES **RHUBARB-INFUSED ST-GERMAIN**
(SEE OPPOSITE)

Place the Meyer lemon juice in an 8-inch-tall container. Add the Sucro and aerate the mixture with an immersion blender, creating a light, bubbly foam.

To serve, pour the rhubarb-infused St-Germain into a 5-ounce champagne flute. Scoop the Meyer lemon air on top until it almost overflows.

RHUBARB-INFUSED ST-GERMAIN

MAKES 1 (750-ML) BOTTLE

6 STALKS **RHUBARB**, CUT INTO ¼-INCH PIECES

1 (750-ML) BOTTLE **ST-GERMAIN ELDERFLOWER LIQUEUR**

Put the rhubarb in a quart-size jar and pour in the St-Germain. Cover and set aside in a cool, dark place to infuse for 1 week. Strain the St-Germain back into the bottle. It will keep for up to 3 months.

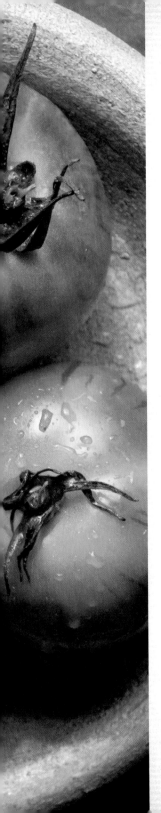

FIRST COURSE

////

The purpose of the first course is to get the juices flowing. I serve something that is not too strong in alcohol but that paves the way for a more substantial cocktail or gets the imbiber thinking about the meal he or she is going to have.

////

Having the flavors of a Margherita pizza come out in a clear liquid is magical, and I thank the great chef Walter Manzke for teaching me how to make it. Adding strawberries makes it a little sweet. • **MAKES 1**

BUBBLY MARY

\\\\\\

3 OUNCES **SPARKLING ROSÉ**

3 OUNCES **CLEAR STRAWBERRY GAZPACHO** (SEE BELOW)

CURRANT TOMATOES ON THE VINE, FOR GARNISH

\\\\\\

Pour the sparkling rosé and gazpacho into a champagne flute and stir with a barspoon. Add the tomatoes so they extend from the bottom to the top of the flute.

CLEAR STRAWBERRY GAZPACHO

MAKES ABOUT 12 OUNCES

1 PINT **GAVIOTA STRAWBERRIES**

2 CLOVES **GARLIC**

5 FRESH **PURPLE BASIL LEAVES**

8 MEDIUM **GREEN ZEBRA TOMATOES**

2 PINCHES OF **SEA SALT**

Combine all the ingredients in a Vitamix or other high-speed blender and pulse until the mixture has a smoothie-like quality. Pour it into a Superbag (see Sources, page 153). Rinse out the blender container, set the Superbag over the top, and let the mixture drip back into the container. The first few drops of liquid are very cloudy, so discard them and let the remaining liquid drip for 3 to 4 hours, or until you have as much as you need. The gazpacho will keep in an airtight container in the refrigerator for up 3 days or in the freezer for up to 6 months.

Yuzu is a Japanese citrus that resembles a cross between a lemon and a lime, and has an explosive and intoxicating aroma. It is used in many forms of sushi and the bottled juice shows up on many restaurant menus. But it is very rare to find it fresh, and there are only a few farms in Southern California that have it available for a few weeks out of the year in early winter. • **MAKES 1**

YUZU

\\\\\

3 BARSPOONS **ALOE VERA CHUNKS**

2 OUNCES **YUZU-INFUSED TEQUILA** (RECIPE FOLLOWS)

¾ OUNCE **AGAVE SYRUP** (RECIPE FOLLOWS)

¾ OUNCE FRESH **LEMON JUICE**

1 OUNCE **CLOVE-INFUSED BLOOD ORANGE JUICE** (RECIPE FOLLOWS)

5 OR 6 **OYSTER BLOSSOMS**

\\\\\

Put the aloe vera chunks in a collins glass and fill the glass with ice. Then pour the tequila, agave, lemon juice, and blood orange juice into a shaker filled with ice, shake, and strain into the glass. Place a boba straw (see Sources, page 153) down the side of the glass and garnish with the oyster blossoms.

YUZU-INFUSED TEQUILA

MAKES 1 (750-ML) BOTTLE

---

7 FRESH **YUZU**

1 (750-ML) BOTTLE **123 ORGANIC BLANCO (UNO) TEQUILA**

Place the yuzu in a 2-quart jar and pour in the tequila. Cover and let sit in a cool, dark place to infuse for 2 weeks. Strain the tequila back into the bottle. It will keep at room temperature for up to 2 months or in the refrigerator for up to 6 months.

CLOVE-INFUSED BLOOD ORANGE JUICE

MAKES ABOUT 4 CUPS

---

4 CUPS FRESH **BLOOD ORANGE JUICE**

2 OUNCES **WHOLE CLOVES**

In a small saucepan, combine the blood orange juice and cloves and bring to a simmer over medium heat. Reduce the heat to medium-low and simmer for 20 minutes, then turn off the heat, cover, and let steep for 1 hour. Strain into a clean container. The infused blood orange juice will keep in the refrigerator for up to 1 week or in the freezer for up to 6 months.

AGAVE SYRUP

MAKES 2 CUPS

In a bowl, combine 1 cup **agave nectar** and 1 cup water. Stir until the agave has dissolved and the mixture is well combined. The agave syrup will keep in an airtight container in the refrigerator for up to 6 months.

Quince is one of those fruits that doesn't have a lot of flavor until you cook it. But there are edible quinces that are really fruity and aromatic even when they are raw, and those are the ones that I like to use. • **MAKES 1 (750-ML) BOTTLE**

QUINCE

〰

5 MEDIUM **QUINCES**

1 (750-ML) BOTTLE **DOLIN BLANC VERMOUTH**

〰

Halve the quinces, place them in a 2-quart jar, and fill to the top with vermouth. Cover and refrigerate for 1 week. Strain the vermouth back into the Dolin bottle, discarding the quinces. The infused vermouth will keep in the refrigerator for up to 1 month.

Pour 3 ounces of the quince-infused vermouth into a shot glass and serve chilled, or heat it up in a saucepan and serve it in a nice teacup and saucer.

I discovered that when I mixed passion fruit and Cappelletti, it tasted a lot like a Greyhound, which is a combination of vodka and grapefruit juice. This similar combination creates a wonderfully bitter and tangy drink that is perfect to start off with. • **MAKES 1**

ITALIAN GREYHOUND

2 OUNCES **CAPPELLETTI VINO APERITIVO AMERICANO ROSSO**

¾ OUNCE **FRESH LIME JUICE**

¾ OUNCE **AGAVE SYRUP** (SEE PAGE 32)

1 OUNCE **PASSION FRUIT PULP**

SMALL GREEN AND RED CHILES, FOR GARNISH

In a cocktail shaker filled with ice, combine the Cappelletti, lime juice, agave, and passion fruit pulp, then shake and strain into a tall glass filled with ice. (A few passion fruit seeds will make their way through the strainer, but this looks great in the glass.) Garnish with a few green and red chiles.

I am not a fan of regular Pimm's, so I wanted to create a version of the Pimm's Cup that I would love. Infusing rhubarb into the base really helps to cut the sweetness and bring out the complexity. • **MAKES 1**

PIMM'S CUP

\\\\\\

¾ OUNCE FRESH **LIME JUICE**

½ OUNCE **AGAVE SYRUP** (SEE PAGE 32)

¼ OUNCE FRESH **GINGER JUICE**

2 SLICES **LEMON CUCUMBER**

3 **SHISO LEAVES**

2 OUNCES **SUMMER PIMM'S INFUSION** (SEE OPPOSITE)

SPRIG OF **FLOWERING WILD FENNEL**

\\\\\\

In a cocktail shaker, muddle the lime juice, agave, ginger juice, lemon cucumber, and shiso leaves. Add the Pimm's infusion and ice, shake, and strain into a wineglass filled with ice. Garnish with the flowering fennel sprig.

SUMMER PIMM'S INFUSION

MAKES 6 CUPS

7 **AVOCADO LEAVES**

4 **RHUBARB STALKS**, DICED

8 **BLENHEIM APRICOTS**, HALVED AND PITTED

2 CUPS **FORDS GIN**

2 CUPS **PUNT E MES**

1 CUP **CHERRY HEERING LIQUEUR**

1 CUP **GRAND MARNIER**

Place the avocado leaves, rhubarb, and apricots in a
2-quart jar and pour in the gin, Punt e Mes, cherry liqueur,
and Grand Marnier. Cover and set aside in a cool, dark
place to infuse for 1 week. Strain into clean glass bottles.
The Pimm's infusion will keep in a cool, dry place for up
to 2 months or in the refrigerator for up to 6 months.

The first time I made a beer cocktail, I wanted to make something that tasted like a fully alcoholic IPA, so I infused cascade hops into gin. Now there is a great hop-infused vodka on the market called Hophead. · **MAKES 1**

CASCADING HOPHEAD

〉〉〉〉〉

2 OUNCES **HOPHEAD VODKA**

¾ OUNCE FRESH **LEMON JUICE**

½ OUNCE FRESH **GRAPEFRUIT JUICE**

½ OUNCE **YELLOW CHARTREUSE**

½ OUNCE **HONEY SYRUP** (SEE PAGE 144)

2 OUNCES **BALLAST POINT SCULPIN IPA**

SPRIG OF **FLOWERING ROSEMARY**, FOR GARNISH

HONEYCOMB SQUARE, FOR GARNISH

〉〉〉〉〉

In a cocktail shaker filled with ice, combine the vodka, lemon juice, grapefruit juice, chartreuse, honey syrup, and IPA, then hold tight and shake. Strain into a pint glass filled with ice and garnish with the flowering rosemary sprig and honeycomb square.

Toyon is a wild berry that grows in California in the late fall. When it's dehydrated, it releases a wonderful cherry flavor. • **MAKES 1**

TOYON

\\\\\

¾ OUNCE FRESH **LIME JUICE**

¾ OUNCE **AGAVE SYRUP** (SEE PAGE 32)

4 OR 5 **WILD WOOD SORREL LEAVES**, PLUS MORE FOR GARNISH

¾ OUNCE **PASTEURIZED EGG WHITES**

2 OUNCES **TOYON BERRY–INFUSED CAPURRO PISCO** (SEE OPPOSITE)

MEADOW SORREL LEAVES, FOR GARNISH (OPTIONAL)

\\\\\

In a cocktail shaker, muddle the lime juice, agave, wood sorrel leaves, and egg whites, then add the infused pisco and shake without ice to emulsify the egg whites. Add ice, shake, double strain into a coupe, and garnish with the wood sorrel and meadow sorrel leaves, if desired.

TOYON BERRY-INFUSED CAPURRO PISCO

MAKES 1 (750-ML) BOTTLE

---

8 OUNCES FRESH **TOYON BERRIES**

1 (750-ML) BOTTLE **CAPURRO PISCO**

Place the toyon berries on a dehydrator tray (see Sources, page 153) and dehydrate for 8 hours. Transfer the berries to a quart-size jar and pour in the pisco. Cover and set aside in a cool, dark place to infuse for 1 week. Strain the pisco back into the bottle. It will keep for up to 3 months.

It's really nice to see how universal and common curry leaves have become. Curry leaves are not necessarily used in curry, and they have an amazing sesame flavor that really goes with the maltiness in the genever. Surinam cherries are indigenous to Brazil and taste like a cherry, red bell pepper, and tomato all in one. One of the most unique flavors I've tried. · **MAKES 1**

THE ONE AND ONLY

\\\\\

¾ OUNCE FRESH **LIME JUICE**

¾ OUNCE **AGAVE SYRUP** (SEE PAGE 32)

SLICE OF **ENGLISH CUCUMBER**

4 **SURINAM CHERRIES**

5 **CURRY LEAVES**, PLUS MORE FOR GARNISH

2 OUNCES **GENEVIEVE GENEVER-STYLE GIN**

\\\\\

In a cocktail shaker, muddle the lime juice, agave, cucumber, Surinam cherries, and curry leaves, then add the genever and ice. Shake, strain into a rocks glass without ice, and garnish with curry leaves.

Hachiya persimmons are the best for cocktails because they are soft and sweet and ready to go, and J.J.'s Lone Daughter Ranch here in California has the best around. I love filling a jar with persimmons and smoking them with a small smoker for about 30 minutes. Breville makes a great smoking gun that comes with different wood chips that you can burn for various smoke flavors. • **MAKES 1**

SMOKED PERSIMMON

¾ OUNCE FRESH **LIME JUICE**

¾ OUNCE **AGAVE SYRUP** (SEE PAGE 32)

1 **SMOKED PERSIMMON** (SEE OPPOSITE)

1 OUNCE **PASSION FRUIT JUICE**

2 OUNCES **ST. GEORGE CALIFORNIA CITRUS VODKA**

DRIED PERSIMMON, FOR GARNISH

In a cocktail shaker, muddle the lime juice, agave, smoked persimmon, and passion fruit juice, then add the vodka and ice. Shake, strain into a rocks glass with ice, and garnish with the dried persimmon.

SMOKED PERSIMMON

MAKES 8 SMOKED PERSIMMONS

Place 8 soft **Hachiya persimmons** in an airtight container. Using a Smoking Gun (see Sources, page 153), fill the container with smoke for 30 seconds. Pull out the smoker and seal the container. Let the smoke infuse the persimmons for 10 minutes, then release the smoke. The persimmons will keep in an airtight container in the refrigerator for up to 5 days.

LAVENDER TEA

MAKES 3 CUPS

Bring 3 cups water to a boil
in a medium saucepan.
Add ½ cup **dried French
lavender buds**. Remove from
the heat and let sit for a
few hours, then strain into
a clean bottle. The tea will
keep for about a week in the
refrigerator.

I was playing around with making a lavender whiskey lemonade when one of my regulars, David Greenberg, suggested adding Cynar. Cynar, a bitter, artichoke-infused liqueur, instantly gave me the profile I was looking for and this became one of my most popular whiskey drinks. • **MAKES 1**

KENTUCKY BUBBLE BATH

////

2 OUNCES **ELIJAH CRAIG 12-YEAR-OLD BOURBON**

¾ OUNCE FRESH **LEMON JUICE**

¾ OUNCE **AGAVE SYRUP** (SEE PAGE 32)

¾ OUNCE **CYNAR**

1 OUNCE **LAVENDER TEA** (SEE OPPOSITE)

2 SPRIGS OF FRESH **LAVENDER**, FOR GARNISH

////

In a cocktail shaker filled with ice, combine the bourbon, lemon juice, agave, Cynar, and lavender tea, then shake and strain into a tall glass with ice. Garnish with the lavender sprigs.

SECOND COURSE

The intention of the second course is to introduce something that is a little more robust in flavor and alcohol but is also a lot more interesting and vibrant. It should ultimately leave the diner completely satisfied and ready to move on to the main course.

This is one of the first drinks I ever created, more than six years ago, and remains to this day my favorite of all of my drinks. I was depressed because I hadn't created a new drink in two weeks and I went down to the walk-in for inspiration and saw some micro arugula. Every time I experiment with a new drink, I muddle a new ingredient on its own with lime juice, agave, and gin to assess the purity of the flavor, and this one did not need to be messed with. It has an outstanding flavor that pairs well with food, especially meat. I came up with the name because in France they call arugula *roquette*. • **MAKES 1**

ROQUETTE

\\\\\

¾ OUNCE FRESH **LIME JUICE**,
PREFERABLY FROM A BEARSS LIME

¾ OUNCE **AGAVE SYRUP** (SEE OPPOSITE)

1 CUP **WILD ARUGULA**,
PREFERABLY RUSTIC (SYLVETTA) ARUGULA

2 OUNCES **CAPROCK GIN**

WILD RADISH FLOWERS OR MICRO ARUGULA,
FOR GARNISH

\\\\\

In a cocktail shaker, muddle the lime juice, agave, and arugula, then add the gin and ice. Shake, then strain into a rocks glass filled with ice and garnish with wild radish flowers or micro arugula.

This is one of the first drinks I created specifically for a wedding. I thought the flavor was very fresh and vibrant, and it was no surprise that it became the most popular drink of the event. The spice and the shiso definitely take your palate in many directions. • MAKES 1

MONKEY SEE MONKEY DO

¾ OUNCE FRESH **LIME JUICE**

¼ OUNCE **AGAVE SYRUP** (SEE PAGE 32)

3 (2-INCH) **WATERMELON CUBES**

3 **PURPLE SHISO LEAVES**

PINCH OF **HEPP'S SALT CO. GHOST PEPPER SEA SALT** (OPTIONAL)

1 OUNCE **CAPROCK GIN**

1 OUNCE **ST-GERMAIN ELDERFLOWER LIQUEUR**

HANDFUL OF **VIOLA FLOWERS**, FOR GARNISH

In a cocktail shaker, muddle the lime juice, agave, watermelon, shiso leaves, and ghost pepper salt (if using), then add the gin, elderflower liqueur, and ice. Shake, then strain into a rocks glass filled with ice and garnish with the violas.

Juicy and fruity, Green Zebra tomatoes are the perfect fruit to muddle for a cocktail. Adding okra to the cachaça creates a grassiness that fuses well with the tomato, leek blossoms, and lovage. If you can't find leek blossoms, use a few small pieces of scallion. Lovage is a summer herb; celery leaves would give a similar flavor profile. And Hepp's ghost pepper sea salt is the perfect way to add spice without the heat interrupting the other flavors. • **MAKES 1**

OKRA AND LOVAGE

\\\\\

¾ OUNCE FRESH **LIME JUICE**

¾ OUNCE **AGAVE SYRUP** (SEE PAGE 32)

4 **LOVAGE LEAVES**

PINCH OF **HEPP'S SALT CO. GHOST PEPPER SEA SALT**

1 MEDIUM **GREEN ZEBRA TOMATO**

10 **LEEK OR SHALLOT BLOSSOMS**

2 OUNCES **OKRA-INFUSED CACHAÇA** (SEE OPPOSITE)

ROOTS OF 3 **SCALLIONS**, FRIED IN **OLIVE OIL** UNTIL CRISPY

CURRANT TOMATOES, FOR GARNISH

\\\\\

In a cocktail shaker, muddle the lime juice, agave, lovage, ghost pepper salt, Green Zebra tomato, and leek blossoms, then add the cachaça and ice. Shake, then strain into a rocks glass filled with ice and garnish with the scallion roots and currant tomatoes.

OKRA-INFUSED CACHAÇA

MAKES 1 (750-ML) BOTTLE

8 OUNCES FRESH **OKRA**

1 (750-ML) BOTTLE **NOVO FOGO SILVER CACHAÇA**

Place the okra in the bottom of a quart-size jar and pour in the cachaça. Cover and set aside in a cool, dark place to infuse for 1 week. Strain the cachaça back into the bottle. It will keep in the refrigerator for up to 3 months.

For this drink, I really wanted to re-create the flavors of the Thai soup *tom kha gai,* and I drew my inspiration from the great bartender Scott Beattie. • **MAKES 1**

LOST IN LAOS

¾ OUNCE FRESH **LIME JUICE**

½ OUNCE **AGAVE SYRUP** (SEE PAGE 32)

½ OUNCE **GREEN CHARTREUSE**

¼ OUNCE **FRESH TURMERIC**

6 **KAFFIR LIME LEAVES**

2 OUNCES **CAPROCK GIN**

2 OUNCES FRESH **COCONUT MILK** (SEE NOTE)

SPRIG OF **FLOWERING THAI BASIL**, FOR GARNISH

In a cocktail shaker, muddle the lime juice, agave, chartreuse, turmeric, and 3 of the kaffir lime leaves, then add the gin, coconut milk, and ice. Shake, then strain into a collins glass filled with ice. To garnish, slide the remaining 3 kaffir lime leaves down the sides of the glass and slide in the sprig of Thai basil on top.

Note: For instructions on making your own coconut milk, visit coconutinformation.com.

I had an incredible cactus taco in Paris a few years ago, and it really left a huge impression on me. I love the grassiness that comes through in this infusion, and I love to make it whenever cactus is in season. • **MAKES 1**

CACTUS SAGE HEAVEN

\\\\\

¾ OUNCE FRESH **LEMON JUICE**

¾ OUNCE **AGAVE SYRUP** (SEE PAGE 32)

5 **GOLDEN RASPBERRIES**

6 FRESH **SAGE LEAVES**

¼ OUNCE FRESH **GINGER JUICE**

2 OUNCES **CACTUS-INFUSED TEQUILA** (SEE OPPOSITE)

SPRIG OF **FLOWERING SAGE**, FOR GARNISH

\\\\\

In a cocktail shaker, muddle the lemon juice, agave, raspberries, 3 of the sage leaves, and the ginger juice, then add the cactus-infused tequila and ice. Shake, then strain into a collins glass. Slide the remaining 3 sage leaves down the sides of the glass and garnish with the flowering sage.

CACTUS-INFUSED TEQUILA

MAKES 2 (750-ML) BOTTLES

---

4 LARGE **CACTUS LEAVES**

2 (750-ML) BOTTLES **123 ORGANIC REPOSADO (DOS) TEQUILA**

Place the cactus leaves in the bottom of a 2-quart jar and pour in the tequila. Cover and set aside in a cool, dark place to infuse for 1 week. Strain the tequila back into the bottles. It will keep in a cool, dark place for up to 3 months.

Years ago, I was encouraged by the producer of Unique Eats to use lovage in a drink, and this was my first attempt. Lovage has an amazing flavor similar to celery, and I now have the Cook's Garden in Venice, California, grow it for me on a yearly basis. The maltiness of the genever brings all the flavors together. • **MAKES 1**

HANKY-PANKY

\\\\\\

½ MEDIUM **PIXIE TANGERINE,** UNPEELED, CUT INTO 4 PIECES

¾ OUNCE FRESH **LIME JUICE**

½ OUNCE **AGAVE SYRUP** (SEE PAGE 32)

½ OUNCE **CAPPELLETTI VINO APERITIVO AMERICANO ROSSO**

4 **LOVAGE LEAVES**

PINCH OF **HEPP'S SALT CO. GHOST PEPPER SALT**

2 OUNCES **GENEVIEVE GENEVER-STYLE GIN**

4 **CORNFLOWER TOPS**, FOR GARNISH

\\\\\\

In a cocktail shaker, muddle the tangerine, lime juice, agave, Cappelletti, lovage, and ghost pepper salt, then add the genever and ice. Shake, then strain into a mini martini or margarita glass without ice and garnish with the cornflowers.

The first time I juiced pumpkins, I knew it was going to be a sad day when they went out of season. The juice has a rich, sweet potato and carrot flavor that is amazing. The Long Island Cheese pumpkin is my favorite. • MAKES 1

PUMPKIN AND PEANUTS

2 OUNCES **PEANUT-INFUSED AQUAVIT** (SEE OPPOSITE)

¾ OUNCE FRESH **LIME JUICE**

¾ OUNCE **AGAVE SYRUP** (SEE PAGE 32)

2 OUNCES FRESH **PUMPKIN JUICE**

HULLED ROASTED **PUMPKIN SEEDS**, FOR GARNISH

In a cocktail shaker filled with ice, combine the peanut-infused aquavit, lime juice, agave, and pumpkin juice. Shake, then strain into a coupe or shot glass and garnish with roasted pumpkin seeds.

PEANUT-INFUSED AQUAVIT

MAKES 1 (750-ML) BOTTLE

2 CUPS UNSHELLED ROASTED PEANUTS

1 (750-ML) BOTTLE KROGSTAD FESTLIG AQUAVIT

Place the peanuts in a quart-size jar and pour in the aquavit. Cover and set aside in a cool, dark place to infuse for 1 week. Strain the aquavit back into the bottle. It will keep in the refrigerator for up to 3 months.

I love combining different spirits, and the two used here have unusual flavors that really dance and sing well together. Clover is an amazing juice company whose products are available nationwide. They make a perfect green juice called The Clover, which pairs really well with this cocktail. • MAKES 1

HEALTH KICK

\\\\\\

1 OUNCE **BENESIN TÓBALA MEZCAL**

1 OUNCE **KROGSTAD FESTLIG AQUAVIT**

¾ OUNCE FRESH **LIME JUICE**

¾ OUNCE **AGAVE SYRUP** (SEE PAGE 32)

1 OUNCE **THE CLOVER GREEN JUICE**
(SEE SOURCES, PAGE 153) OR FRESH CELERY JUICE

PINCH OF **HIMALAYAN SEA SALT**

NASTURTIUM BLOSSOMS AND **WILD MUSTARD FLOWERS**,
FOR GARNISH

\\\\\\

In a shaker filled with ice, combine the mezcal, aquavit, lime juice, agave, green juice, and salt. Shake, then double strain into a collins glass. Submerge the nasturtium flowers in the drink and garnish with the wild mustard flowers.

I love the silky creaminess of unfiltered sake and wanted to create something that had a cereal flavor to it. The pear brandy from CapRock is extraordinary, so I tried pairing it with sake. • **MAKES 1**

SWEET BITTER END OF TOKYO

\\\\\

¾ OUNCE FRESH **LIME JUICE**

¾ OUNCE **AGAVE SYRUP** (SEE PAGE 32)

⅓ MEDIUM **ASIAN PEAR**, CORED

2 PINCHES OF CHOPPED FRESH **DILL**

1 OUNCE **MOCHI-INFUSED BRANDY** (SEE OPPOSITE)

1 OUNCE **ROCK SAKÉ CLOUD**

SPRIG OF FRESH **DILL**, FOR GARNISH

\\\\\

In a cocktail shaker, muddle the lime juice, agave, pear, and chopped dill, then add the infused brandy, sake, and ice. Shake, then double strain into a rocks glass with ice and garnish with the sprig of dill.

MOCHI-INFUSED BRANDY

MAKES 2 (375-ML) BOTTLES

---

5 **SWEET BROWN RICE MOCHI** (RICE CAKES)

2 (375-ML) BOTTLES **CAPROCK PEAR BRANDY**

Crumble the mochi into a quart-size jar and pour in the brandy. Cover and set aside in a cool, dark place to infuse for 10 days. Strain the brandy back into the bottle. It will keep in the refrigerator for up to 3 months.

MAIN COURSE

////

The main course should consist of a cocktail that can stand on its own, something that makes people feel that they are getting a whole meal compressed into a glass.

////

One night, one of my customers saw that I was using beet horseradish in my seventeen-step Bloody Mary and asked me if I could make a different drink with the horseradish. So I just made a very simple cucumber gin gimlet and added a barspoon of the horseradish to it. This is a perfect drink for people who don't like Bloody Marys but still want something savory. • **MAKES 1**

BREEDERS' CUP

///\\\

¾ OUNCE FRESH **LIME JUICE**

¾ OUNCE **AGAVE SYRUP** (SEE PAGE 32)

3 **CUCUMBER ROUNDS**, ⅛ INCH THICK,
PLUS MORE FOR GARNISH

1 BARSPOON **BEET HORSERADISH** (SEE OPPOSITE),
OR PREPARED BEET HORSERADISH, SUCH AS BUBBIES

2 OUNCES **CAPROCK GIN**

PINCH OF **HEPP'S SALT CO. APPLEWOOD SMOKED
SEA SALT** (SEE SOURCES, PAGE 153), FOR GARNISH

HANDFUL OF **BORAGE FLOWERS**, FOR GARNISH

///\\\

In a cocktail shaker, muddle the lime juice, agave, cucumber, and beet horseradish, then add the gin and ice. Shake, then strain into a rocks glass filled with ice. Garnish with the smoked salt, borage flowers, and cucumber slices.

BEET HORSERADISH

MAKES ABOUT 7 OUNCES

---

1 (5-OUNCE) JAR **HORSERADISH**
(PREFERABLY BUBBIES; SEE SOURCES, PAGE 153)

¼ CUP FRESH **RED BEET JUICE**

In a pint jar, combine the horseradish and beet juice.
Cover and set aside for 1 hour. The horseradish will
keep in the refrigerator for up to 3 days but is best used
the day after preparation. (Alternatively, Bubbies makes
a great prepared beet horseradish.)

I was doing an uni dinner with a bunch of chefs in downtown Los Angeles and knew I had to attempt an uni drink that would pair with the meal. The trick was turning the uni into a puree so it would mix well, and I have Brian Huskey, runner-up on season 11 of *Top Chef,* to thank for that. • **MAKES 1**

UNI

\\\\\

¾ OUNCE **CUMIN SIMPLE SYRUP** (RECIPE FOLLOWS)

¾ OUNCE FRESH **LEMON JUICE**

1 OUNCE **UNI PUREE** (RECIPE FOLLOWS)

3 OR 4 MEDIUM **STRAWBERRIES**

2 PINCHES OF FRESH **MARJORAM**

2 OUNCES **123 ORGANIC REPOSADO (DOS) TEQUILA**

SPRIG OF **FLOWERING MARJORAM** (FOR GARNISH)

\\\\\

In a cocktail shaker, muddle the cumin simple syrup, lemon juice, uni puree, strawberries, and marjoram. Add the tequila and ice. Shake, then strain into a rocks glass filled with ice. Garnish with the flowering marjoram.

CUMIN SIMPLE SYRUP

MAKES ABOUT 1 CUP

---

1 CUP **SUGAR**

3 TABLESPOONS GROUND **CUMIN**

In a small saucepan, combine the sugar, cumin, and
1 cup water. Bring to a simmer over medium heat,
stirring until the sugar has dissolved. Remove from the
heat and let cool, then transfer to an airtight container.
The syrup will keep in the refrigerator for up to 1 week.

UNI PUREE

Adapted from Chefs Brian Huskey and Jason Park.

---

500 GRAMS **UNI**

⅛ TEASPOON **SEA SALT**

Create a bain-marie by setting a stainless-steel bowl over a saucepan filled with a few inches of water. The water should not touch the bottom of the bowl. Bring the water to a simmer over medium heat. Fill a large bowl with ice and set aside.

Combine the uni, salt, and 1¾ cups water in a food processor and process to remove all lumps.

Transfer the mixture to the bowl over the saucepan and cook slowly over the simmering water.

When the mixture is thick enough to coat the back of a spoon, put the bowl on the ice bath to stop the cooking. Continue to stir. When the custard has cooled enough so that there is no steam rising, strain through a fine-mesh sieve into a container and reserve at room temperature until ready to use, or let cool until ice cold and store in the refrigerator for up to 2 days.

Having grown up in New England, I have oysters and cherrystone clams deep in my memory bank. And I love the idea of using the whole oyster and shell as the vessel for the cocktail. The brine from seafood goes really well with smoky and peaty Scotch—Erik Lund, who was the bar manager at MessHall Kitchen in Los Angeles, turned me on to that combination. • MAKES 1

OYSTER

1 OUNCE **LAPHROAIG 10-YEAR-OLD SCOTCH**

1 **SHUCKED OYSTER** OF YOUR CHOICE, PREFERABLY WITH A DEEP SHELL

1 TEASPOON **GHEE**, MELTED

ALOE FOAM (SEE OPPOSITE)

GARLIC BLOSSOMS, FOR GARNISH

Pour the Scotch on top of the oyster, then add the ghee. Top it off with aloe foam and a sprinkle of garlic blossoms.

ALOE FOAM

MAKES 15 SERVINGS

---

1 CUP **CHAREAU ALOE VERA LIQUEUR**

1 CUP **EGG WHITES**

2 TABLESPOONS **WHEATGRASS JUICE**

In an iSi cream whipper (see Sources, page 153), combine the aloe vera liqueur, egg whites, and wheatgrass juice and seal. Charge the canister with two N_2O cartridges, shake, and refrigerate overnight before using. It will keep for up to 1 week.

When I started at the Library Bar, it was at the beginning of this whole cocktail movement, and it was really important to make a great cocktail that was going to have a strong point of reference to people. So I set out to make the best Bloody Mary I could, because if I could get people to love it, then they would trust me with my more experimental cocktails. • **MAKES 1**

MOTHER MARY

¾ OUNCE FRESH **LIME JUICE**

¾ OUNCE FRESH **LEMON JUICE**

¾ OUNCE **OLIVE JUICE** (FROM A JAR OF OLIVES)

PINCH OF **DILL**

PINCH OF **CILANTRO**

3 OR 4 DICED **RED BELL PEPPER** PIECES

3 SLICES **ENGLISH CUCUMBER**

3 OR 4 **CHERRY TOMATOES**

7 OR 8 CHOPPED **SCALLION** PIECES

2 OUNCES **KROGSTAD FESTLIG AQUAVIT**

1 BARSPOON **BEET HORSERADISH** (SEE PAGE 71)
OR PREPARED BEET HORSERADISH, SUCH AS BUBBIES

1 OUNCE **STIRRINGS BLOODY MARY MIX**

SPRIG OF **FLOWERING GARLIC CHIVES**, FOR GARNISH

YELLOW CHERRY TOMATO, FOR GARNISH

FRIED SQUASH BLOSSOM, FOR GARNISH

In a cocktail shaker, muddle the lime juice, lemon juice, olive juice, dill, cilantro, pepper pieces, cucumber, tomatoes, and scallion, then add the aquavit, horseradish, and Bloody Mary mix. Add ice, and with two larger shakers, roll the liquid back and forth five or six times to mix properly. Do not shake. You don't want a Bloody Mary to get frothy from shaking. Pour the Bloody Mary into a glass filled with ice and garnish with the flowering chives, cherry tomato, and squash blossom.

A gin and tonic was the first cocktail I ever had, and it stayed with me for years. Here, the the smoky meatiness of mezcal combined with the juniper berries brings on the ultimate savory sensation. The more this drink sits, the more robust it gets. • **MAKES 1**

MEZCAL AND TONIC

2 OUNCES **JUNIPER-INFUSED MEZCAL** (SEE OPPOSITE)

3 OUNCES **FEVER-TREE ELDERFLOWER TONIC**

3 **KUMQUATS**, SLICED

2 PINCHES OF CHOPPED FRESH **DILL**

4 CHOPPED **LEEK** PIECES

4 **KALAMATA OLIVES**

FRESH **LIME JUICE**

CRACKED **BLACK PEPPER**

FENNEL FROND, FOR GARNISH

Combine the mezcal, tonic, kumquats, dill, leek, and olives in a wide stemless wineglass and stir. Squeeze in a bit of lime juice and sprinkle with cracked black pepper. Garnish with the fennel frond and serve.

JUNIPER-INFUSED MEZCAL

MAKES 1 (750-ML) BOTTLE

---

2 OUNCES **JUNIPER BERRIES**

1 (750-ML) BOTTLE **BENESIN TOBALA MEZCAL**

Place the juniper berries in a quart-size jar and pour in the mezcal. Cover and set aside in a cool, dark place to infuse for 1 week. Strain the mezcal back into the bottle. It will keep in a cool, dark place for up to 6 months.

This drink tastes like a pepperoni pizza with a nice amount of spice on top; it elevates a dirty martini. Manzanilla sherry has some wonderful olive notes that complement this well. • **MAKES 1**

DIRTY SICILIAN

3 OUNCES **MONKEY 47 GIN**

1 OUNCE **GARLIC-INFUSED SHERRY** (RECIPE FOLLOWS)

¾ OUNCE **OLIVE JUICE** (FROM A JAR OF OLIVES)

3 **FETA-STUFFED OLIVES** (RECIPE FOLLOWS)

2 PINCHES OF **RED PEPPER FLAKES**

1 PINCH OF FRESH **OREGANO LEAVES**

In a mixing glass, combine the gin, sherry, and olive juice. Add ice and stir quickly for 7 seconds. Strain into a coupe or martini glass and garnish with the olives, red pepper flakes, and oregano.

GARLIC-INFUSED SHERRY

MAKES 1 (750-ML) BOTTLE

3 OR 4 **GARLIC CLOVES**

1 (750-ML) BOTTLE **MANZANILLA SHERRY**

Chop the garlic and place it in the bottle of sherry. Cover and refrigerate for 3 days to infuse the sherry. (Sherry is a wine that needs to be refrigerated as soon as it's opened.) Strain the sherry into a clean bottle and store in the refrigerator for up to 3 months.

FETA-STUFFED OLIVES

MAKES ABOUT 1 CUP

8 OUNCES **FETA CHEESE**

½ CUP **EXTRA-VIRGIN OLIVE OIL**

FRESHLY GROUND **BLACK PEPPER**

1 (8-OUNCE) JAR PITTED **GREEN OLIVES**

Crumble the feta into a bowl. Add the olive oil and pepper to taste and mix well. Set aside on the counter for a few hours until the feta softens. Drain the olives, then stuff them with the feta mixture. Store the stuffed olives in an airtight container in the refrigerator for up to 3 months.

When I was first reading about umami flavors years ago, one of the examples I would always see were shiitakes, so I wanted to make a Manhattan with them. The CapRock bitter is a wine-based amaro and is one of the only biodynamic spirits on the market in the U.S. • **MAKES 1**

SHIITAKE

2 OUNCES **MUSHROOM-INFUSED BOURBON** (SEE BELOW)

½ OUNCE **CYNAR**

½ OUNCE **CAPROCK BITTER**

Pour the mushroom-infused bourbon, Cynar, and bitter into a mixing glass with ice. Stir, then strain into a cordial glass.

MUSHROOM-INFUSED BOURBON

MAKES 1 (750-ML) BOTTLE

2 OUNCES FRESH **SHIITAKE MUSHROOMS**

1 (750-ML) BOTTLE **BASIL HAYDEN'S BOURBON**

Place the mushrooms in a quart-size jar and pour in the bourbon. Cover and set aside in a cool, dark place to infuse for 5 days. The flavor should be good and strong by then. Strain the bourbon back into the bottle. It will keep in the refrigerator for up to 3 months.

Bonito flakes are made from the smoked or air-dried belly of skipjack tuna and are used to make dashi. They have the perfect balance of smokiness and fishiness that blends really well with Scotch and citrus.

FISH OUT OF WATER

\\\\\\

¾ OUNCE FRESH **LEMON JUICE**

¾ OUNCE **AGAVE SYRUP** (SEE PAGE 32)

3 GREEN **SHISO LEAVES**

2 OUNCES **BONITO-INFUSED BLENDED SCOTCH**
(SEE OPPOSITE)

4 DROPS **OLIVE OIL**, FOR GARNISH

ONION SPROUTS, FOR GARNISH

\\\\\\

In a cocktail shaker, muddle the lemon juice, agave, and shiso leaves, then add the Scotch and ice. Shake, then double strain into a coupe. Top with the olive oil drops and a handful of the onion sprouts.

BONITO-INFUSED BLENDED SCOTCH

MAKE 1 (750-ML) BOTTLE

---

2 OUNCES **BONITO FLAKES**
1 (750-ML) BOTTLE **BANK NOTE BLENDED SCOTCH**

Place the bonito flakes in a quart-size jar and pour in the Scotch. Cover and set aside in a cool, dark place to infuse for 3 days. Strain the Scotch back into the bottle. It will keep in the refrigerator for up to 2 months.

The homemade sriracha from Windrose Farm in Paso Robles, California, is insane. It's made from smoked jalapeños and tomatoes to deliver the perfect amount of heat and smoke. Because of the intensity of the flavor, it makes sense to serve this as a shot for up to five people. • **MAKES 5**

WHOLE ENCHILADA

1 OUNCE **MEZCAL**

1 OUNCE **123 ORGANIC REPOSADO (DOS) TEQUILA**

¾ OUNCE FRESH **LIME JUICE**

¾ OUNCE **AGAVE SYRUP** (SEE PAGE 32)

1 OUNCE FRESH **PASSION FRUIT PULP** OR FRESH **BLOOD ORANGE JUICE**

1 BARSPOON **WINDROSE SHADES OF HADES SRIRACHA** (RECIPE FOLLOWS)

YELLOW MARIGOLD FLOWERS, FOR GARNISH

In a cocktail shaker, mix the mezcal, tequila, lime juice, agave, passion fruit pulp, and sriracha together with ice. Shake, then strain into five 4-inch test tubes and garnish with marigold flowers.

WINDROSE SHADES OF HADES SRIRACHA

*This recipe makes a somewhat thick sauce; if you'd like
it more flowable, adding more water at the start is best,
but you can add distilled or boiled water later.*

MAKES 3 CUPS

1½ POUNDS RIPE **RED JALAPEÑOS**,
SEEDED, DEVEINED, AND COARSELY CHOPPED

1¼ POUNDS **FARM-SMOKED DRIED HEIRLOOM TOMATOES**,
LEFT WHOLE

1 HEAD **HARDNECK GARLIC**,
CLOVES PEELED AND FINELY CHOPPED

¼ CUP **RAW BROWN SUGAR**

1 TABLESPOON **SEA SALT**

½ CUP **RED OR WHITE WINE VINEGAR**

In a medium saucepan, combine all the ingredients
with ¼ cup water and bring to a simmer over low to
medium heat. Stir to dissolve the sugar and salt, using
additional water if needed. Simmer for 45 minutes to
1 hour, or until the dried tomatoes have become very
loose and pliable. The mixture should start to darken
slightly. Turn off the heat and let the sauce rest. While
the sauce is still hot to warm, transfer it to a Vitamix or
other high-speed blender and blend for 2 to 4 minutes,
until no visible pieces of tomato remain. (Alternatively,
you can blend the sauce directly in the saucepan using
an immersion blender.) Transfer the sauce to jars or
bottles and refrigerate for up to 6 months.

WHITE PEPPERCORN-INFUSED GIN

MAKES 1 (750-ML) BOTTLE

---

1 CUP **WHOLE WHITE PEPPERCORNS,** PREFERABLY SARAWAK

1 (750-ML) BOTTLE **CAPROCK GIN**

Place the peppercorns in a quart-size jar and pour in the gin. Cover and set aside in a cool, dark place to infuse for 3 days. Strain the gin back into the bottle. It will keep in the refrigerator for up to 3 months.

Tomato and basil is such a classic combination, and white pepper comes in many different varieties with distinct flavors. Sarawak white peppercorns from Malaysian Borneo are considered "extra fancy." The berries are large and flavorful, with a uniform creamy white color and hot flavor. • **MAKES 1**

FELLINI'S INSALADA

////

¾ OUNCE FRESH **LIME JUICE**

½ OUNCE **AGAVE SYRUP** (SEE PAGE 32)

½ OUNCE **BALSAMIC VINEGAR**

3 **CHERRY TOMATOES**

2 FRESH **BASIL LEAVES**

2 OUNCES **WHITE PEPPERCORN–INFUSED GIN**
(SEE OPPOSITE)

FLOWERING PURPLE OPAL BASIL, FOR GARNISH

CHERRY TOMATOES, FOR GARNISH

CRUSHED ICE, FOR GARNISH

////

In a cocktail shaker, muddle the lime juice, agave, vinegar, cherry tomatoes, and basil leaves, then add the gin and ice. Shake, then strain into a martini glass. Garnish with the flowering basil, cherry tomatoes, and crushed ice.

DESSERT

〉〉〉〉〉

Dessert is dessert. Rich, creamy,
and decadent and all of that can
be incorporated into cocktails.
This course, like the main
course, can easily stand on its
own as a substantial replacement
for any dessert.

〉〉〉〉〉

This is the drink that I am most proud of because it was the first drink I made that broke the general rule of using spirit, sugar, and citrus. I knew I wanted St-Germain to be the first foam I ever made and the great bartender Vincenzo Marianella instructed me on how to create it. And what is great about using an aged balsamic vinegar is that it carries both the citrus and sweet components needed for the cocktail. • **MAKES 1**

THE LAST TANGO IN MODENA

\\\\\

4 **STRAWBERRIES**

1 OUNCE **25-YEAR-OLD TRADITIONAL BALSAMIC VINEGAR**, PREFERABLY LEONARDO E ROBERTO'S GOURMET BLENDS

2 OUNCES **HENDRICK'S GIN**

ST-GERMAIN FOAM (SEE OPPOSITE)

SLICE OF FRESH **STRAWBERRY**, FOR GARNISH

\\\\\

In a cocktail shaker, muddle the strawberries and vinegar, then add the gin and ice. Shake, then strain into a Quaffer glass (see Sources, page 153) without ice or a rocks glass filled with ice. Top with the St-Germain foam and garnish with the strawberry slice.

ST-GERMAIN FOAM

MAKES 15 SERVINGS

---

1 CUP **ST-GERMAIN**

1 CUP **EGG WHITES**

In an iSi cream whipper (see Sources, page 153), combine the St-Germain and egg whites and seal. Charge the canister with two N_2O cartridges, shake, and refrigerate overnight before using. The foam will keep in the cream whipper in the refrigerator for up to 1 week.

Candy Cap mushrooms were discovered in Northern California about fifteen years ago and are in season for only two weeks out of the year. But what makes them so special is that when dried, they release an amino acid that gives off the flavors of maple syrup and burnt sugar, which I thought would be perfect for ice cream. • **MAKES 1**

CANDY CAP MUSHROOM BOURBON ICE CREAM

2 SCOOPS **CANDY CAP BOURBON ICE CREAM** (RECIPE FOLLOWS)

1 OUNCE **NOCINO** (PAGE 131)

HANDFUL OF **SHELLED WALNUTS**

8 **ROSEMARY BLOSSOMS**, WITH OR WITHOUT SPRIG

Place the ice cream in a bowl, pour the nocino over the top, and garnish with the walnuts and rosemary blossoms. Serve with a spoon.

CANDY CAP BOURBON ICE CREAM

Adapted from Heather Christensen, pastry chef at GreenFire Restaurant in Rockford, Illinois, where I consulted in 2012.

MAKES ABOUT 1 QUART

1 OUNCE DRIED **CANDY CAP MUSHROOMS**

1 (750-ML) BOTTLE **BASIL HAYDEN'S BOURBON**

1½ CUPS **WHOLE MILK**

2 CUPS **HEAVY CREAM**

¼ CUP **SUGAR**

½ TEASPOON **SEA SALT**

6 **EGG YOLKS**

2 TABLESPOONS **VANILLA EXTRACT**

Place the mushrooms in a quart-size glass jar and pour the bourbon over them. Set aside in a cool, dark place to infuse for 1 week, then strain into a clean bottle.

When ready to make the ice cream, combine the milk, cream, sugar, and salt in a large saucepan and cook, stirring frequently, over medium heat. Put the yolks in a heatproof bowl and whisk lightly. When the cream mixture is starting to steam and tiny bubbles have formed along the edge, whisk 1 cup or so of the cream mixture, ¼ cup at a time, into the yolks to temper them. Once the eggs are tempered, slowly whisk them into the saucepan with the remaining cream mixture. Cook over low heat, stirring continuously, for about 5 minutes, until the cream mixture has thickened enough to coat the back of a wooden spoon. Turn off the heat and stir in the vanilla and ½ cup of the mushroom-infused bourbon (reserve the remaining bourbon for another use).

Pour the custard into a large bowl set over a bowl of ice and water until cold. Cover the custard with plastic wrap, pressing it directly against the surface to prevent a skin from forming, and chill for a long time—5 hours or more is optimal.

Transfer the chilled custard to an ice cream maker and churn according to the manufacturer's instructions, noting that the ice cream could be quite runny after 20 to 30 minutes of churning. Spoon the ice cream into an airtight container and freeze for as long as you can, preferably overnight for a well-cured scoop.

White truffles are not for everyone, but to me they are the king of umami. After one of my regulars told me about a white truffle milk shake he had at a seminar with Grant Achatz, the famous chef from Alinea, I knew I wanted to make an eggnog with the four-thousand-dollar-a-pound mushroom from Alba, Italy. • **MAKES 1**

WHITE TRUFFLE EGGNOG

\\\\\\

2 OUNCES **COGNAC PARK COGNAC**

2 OUNCES **WHITE TRUFFLE–INFUSED CREAM** (RECIPE FOLLOWS)

1 OUNCE **AGAVE SYRUP** (SEE PAGE 32)

1 **EGG**

DARK CHOCOLATE SHAVINGS, FOR GARNISH

WHITE TRUFFLE SHAVINGS, FOR GARNISH

\\\\\\

Put the cognac, white truffle–infused cream, agave, and egg in a cocktail shaker. Shake for 10 seconds, then add ice, shake, and double strain into a hollowed-out emu egg (see Note, page 106) or a glass of your choice, without ice. Garnish with the dark chocolate and white truffle shavings.

WHITE TRUFFLE-INFUSED CREAM

MAKES 2 CUPS

1 GOLF-BALL-SIZE **WHITE TRUFFLE**, QUARTERED

2 CUPS **HEAVY CREAM**

Place the truffle in a quart-size jar and pour in the heavy cream. Cover and refrigerate for 3 to 5 days, depending on the strength of the aroma you desire. Use immediately for maximum freshness.

Note: Emus are the largest bird native to Australia and the second largest flightless bird in the world next to the ostrich, which is indigenous to Africa. Both have been domesticated here in Southern California, ostriches for their meat and emus for their eggs and eggshells. Both eggs are equally beautiful and majestic, but I find the flavor of the ostrich egg to be a little too gamy.

When I discovered emu eggs from Schaner Farms near San Diego, I was instantly in love. They have such a beautiful smooth texture and flavor, as if someone already injected them with cream or butter. But it is their incredible natural aqua-colored shell that makes this egg magnificent.

To use the emu egg as a vessel for serving this cocktail, use a Dremel rotary tool to carefully cut off the top of the eggshell. Rest the bottom in a wide glass before pouring in the drink.

Cacao, the plant from which chocolate is made, was first cultivated by the ancient Mayans. Their preferred method of consumption for chocolate was as a thick, bitter, frothy drink served cold. I prefer to make a chocolate syrup that is thick; adding a bit of spice and smoke transports it to another place, how I imagine the Yucatán to taste and feel. • **MAKES 1**

MAYAN CAMPFIRE

\\\\\\

2 OUNCES **123 ORGANIC REPOSADO (DOS) TEQUILA**

2 OUNCES **CHOCOLATE SYRUP** (RECIPE FOLLOWS)

1 BARSPOON **SMOKED JALAPEÑO TEQUILA**
(RECIPE FOLLOWS)

5 OR 6 **MARSHMALLOWS** (RECIPE FOLLOWS),
FOR GARNISH

\\\\\\

In a cocktail shaker, combine the tequila, chocolate syrup, and smoked jalapeño tequila with ice. Shake, then strain into a rocks glass filled with ice. Place the marshmallows on top and slowly toast them with a small kitchen torch (see Sources, page 153). Be very careful not to apply the flame for too long on any one area near the rim of the glass. The whole process should take less than 10 seconds.

MARSHMALLOWS

Adapted from Martha Stewart.

MAKES 24 MARSHMALLOWS

VEGETABLE OIL, FOR BRUSHING

3 CUPS **GRANULATED SUGAR**

1¼ CUPS **LIGHT CORN SYRUP**

¼ TEASPOON **SALT**

4 (¼-OUNCE) ENVELOPES **UNFLAVORED GELATIN**

2 TEASPOONS PURE **VANILLA EXTRACT**

1½ CUPS **CONFECTIONERS' SUGAR**

Brush a 9-by-13-inch glass baking dish with oil. Line the dish with parchment paper, leaving a 2-inch overhang on the long sides. Brush the parchment paper with oil.

In a medium saucepan, combine the granulated sugar, corn syrup, salt, and ¾ cup water. Bring to a boil over high heat, stirring to dissolve the sugar. Clip a candy thermometer to the side of the pan and cook, without stirring, until the mixture registers 238°F, about 9 minutes.

Meanwhile, put ¾ cup cold water in the bowl of a stand mixer and sprinkle the gelatin over the surface. Let the gelatin soften for 5 minutes.

Fit the mixer with the whisk attachment and with the mixer on low speed, slowly stream the hot sugar syrup into the gelatin mixture. Gradually raise the speed to high and beat until the mixture is very stiff, about 12 minutes. Add the vanilla. Pour the mixture into the prepared dish and smooth the top with an offset spatula. Set aside, uncovered, until firm, about 3 hours.

Sift 1 cup of the confectioners' sugar onto a work surface. Unmold the marshmallow onto the confectioners' sugar and remove the parchment. Lightly brush a sharp knife with oil, then cut the marshmallow into 2-inch squares, oiling the knife again as necessary to prevent the marshmallows from sticking. Sift the remaining ½ cup confectioners' sugar into a small bowl and roll each marshmallow in the sugar to coat. The marshmallows can be stored in an airtight container at room temperature for up to 3 days.

CHOCOLATE SYRUP

MAKES ABOUT 2½ CUPS

In a small saucepan, combine 2 cups **Amedei hot chocolate powder** (see Sources, page 153) and 1 cup water. Heat over medium heat until the chocolate powder has fully dissolved and the syrup is rich.

SMOKED JALAPEÑO TEQUILA

MAKES 1 (750-ML) BOTTLE

10 **SMOKED JALAPEÑOS**

1 (750-ML) BOTTLE **123 ORGANIC REPOSADO (DOS) TEQUILA**

Place the jalapeños in a quart-size jar and pour in the tequila. Cover and let sit in a cool, dark place to infuse for at least 2 weeks. Strain back into the bottle. This infusion becomes so strong with smoke and spice that it is intended to be a tincture and not consumed on its own. It will keep in a cool, dark place for at least a year.

Chai is such a unique and distinct flavor and I wanted to create an iced tea made in the same vein as a Vietnamese coffee. This is an easy combination to re-create and is definitely a rich dessert drink. • **MAKES 3 TO 4**

CHAI ICED TEA

2 OUNCES **CHAI-INFUSED GIN** (SEE BELOW)

2 OUNCES **CONDENSED MILK**

3 OR 4 **CINNAMON STICKS**, FOR GARNISH

Into a cocktail shaker with ice, pour the chai-infused gin and condensed milk, shake, and then strain into 3 or 4 shot glasses. Garnish each with a cinnamon stick.

CHAI-INFUSED GIN

MAKES 1 (750-ML) BOTTLE

2 TABLESPOONS **DRIED CHAI TEA**

1 (750-ML) BOTTLE **CAPROCK GIN**

Put the chai directly into the bottle of gin. Let it steep for about 1 hour, agitating it every 15 minutes, and then strain into a clean bottle. Tea is one of the few things that can overinfuse in alcohol, so it's really important to watch this carefully. The infused gin will keep in a cool, dark place for up to 6 months.

Apples are gold on the East Coast, where I grew up. There is nothing like a great Cortland. Having been away for almost twenty-five years, I have grown to love the Honeycrisp for its sweet but tart flavor and the amazing crispness that is consistent every time. A frozen apple also makes a great ice cube, and one that won't dilute your drink. • **MAKES 1**

MEXICAN APPLE PIE

⅓ **HONEYCRISP OR FUJI APPLE**, CORED

¾ OUNCE FRESH **LEMON JUICE**

¾ OUNCE **CINNAMON-HONEY SYRUP** (RECIPE FOLLOWS)

2 OUNCES **123 ORGANIC AÑEJO (TRES) TEQUILA**

1 **APPLE CUBE** (RECIPE FOLLOWS)

3 **DEHYDRATED APPLE SLICES** (RECIPE FOLLOWS), FOR GARNISH

In a cocktail shaker, muddle the apple, lemon juice, and honey syrup, then add the tequila. Shake, then strain over the apple cube in a rocks glass and garnish with the dehydrated apple slices.

CINNAMON-HONEY SYRUP

MAKES 4 CUPS

3 CUPS **WILDFLOWER HONEY**

2 TABLESPOONS GROUND VIETNAMESE **CINNAMON**

In a small saucepan, bring 1 cup water to a boil. Turn off the heat and add the honey. Stir until the honey has completely dissolved. Add the cinnamon, mix well, and let cool. Pour the syrup into a clean jar. It will keep in the refrigerator for up to 1 month.

APPLE CUBES

MAKES 6 APPLE CUBES

Place 6 small **Honeycrisp** or **Fuji apples**, sitting upright, in large freezer bags and place them in the freezer for at least 24 hours. Use the apple cubes within a week of freezing.

DEHYDRATED APPLE SLICES

MAKES ABOUT 18 APPLE SLICES

Cut 3 medium **Honeycrisp** or **Fuji apples** crosswise into ⅛-inch-thick slices. Core the slices, then arrange on dehydrator trays (see Sources, page 153) and dehydrate for 8 hours. Transfer to a plastic freezer bag and store in a cool, dry place. The apple slices will keep for up to 3 months.

I am a huge fan of SelvaRey rum, particularly their cacao rum. It's made in Panama and aged for five years in bourbon barrels and has the most amazing chocolate flavor without being too sweet. The rum, in combination with the peaches and basil, makes this a really great mojito. • **MAKES 1**

TOOTSIE ROLL OVER

¾ OUNCE FRESH **LIME JUICE**

¾ OUNCE **AGAVE SYRUP** (SEE PAGE 32)

⅓ **YELLOW PEACH**, UNPEELED

3 FRESH **BASIL LEAVES**

2 OUNCES **SELVAREY CACAO RUM**

SPRIGS OF **FLOWERING OREGANO**, FOR GARNISH

In a cocktail shaker, muddle the lime juice, agave, peach, and basil leaves, then add the rum. Shake, then strain into a rocks glass without ice. Garnish with flowering oregano.

AFTER DINNER

I love to serve spirited drinks after a meal to balance everything out. Also, a nice selection of homemade liqueurs and cocktails with digestifs are a perfect way to end the meal but still leave you feeling light and satisfied. They should complement the desserts and respect what your palate's last memory should be.

This is an amazing grapefruit liqueur that is fun to make and great to sip on after dinner. · **MAKES 6 TO 8 LITERS**

VIN DE PAMPLEMOUSSE

\\\\

10 **BERGAMOT ORANGES**

6 MEDIUM **RUBY RED GRAPEFRUITS**
(THE DEEPER RED, THE BETTER)

3 CUPS **SUGAR**

2 CUPS DRIED OR FRESH **CHAMOMILE**

2 **VANILLA BEANS**

5 LITERS **DRY WHITE WINE**
(I PREFER SANCERRE OR ANY WHITE
FROM THE LOIRE VALLEY)

2 (750-ML) BOTTLES **123 ORGANIC
BLANCO (UNO) TEQUILA**

\\\\

Wash the oranges and grapefruits well and then slice them into ½-inch-thick rounds. Remove the seeds, as they will add an unpleasant bitterness to the end product.

(recipe continues)

Pack the citrus slices into a 2½-gallon glass jar, sprinkling the sugar and the chamomile flowers between the layers as you go.

Split the vanilla beans lengthwise and add them to the jar.

Pour the wine and tequila over the fruit. Stir well with a long-handled spoon, getting all the way to the bottom of the jar.

Seal the jar and tuck it into the corner of a dark closet. For the first week, visit the jar and give it a good stir every day to make sure the sugar fully dissolves.

After 40 days, strain the mixture and discard the citrus, vanilla beans, and chamomile. Line a fine-mesh sieve with cheesecloth and strain the mixture twice more, then funnel the elixir into 6 to 8 clean 1-liter bottles.

Store away from direct sunlight and heat. The finished vin will keep indefinitely.

When I was consulting for the Almond Board of California a few years ago, I had to create cocktails using almonds and found that roasted almond oil was a great replacement for a sweetener, especially if you are working with a liqueur that already has some sugar in it. • **MAKES 1**

NUTTY MONK

\\\\\\

2 OUNCES **BÉNÉDICTINE**

¾ OUNCE **LA TOURANGELLE ROASTED ALMOND OIL**

¾ OUNCE FRESH **LEMON JUICE**

CACAO NIBS, FOR GARNISH

\\\\\\

In a cocktail shaker with ice, combine the Bénédictine, roasted almond oil, and lemon juice. Shake, then double strain into a coupe without ice and garnish with the cacao nibs.

Un caffè va bene is Italian for "have a coffee, everything is good." This coffee drink is great any time of day, but is also a wonderful digestif. The inclusion of Cynar creates a really long finish. • **MAKES 1**

UN CAFFÈ VA BENE

\\\\\\

2 OUNCES **CYNAR**

½ OUNCE **CRÈME DE CASSIS**

1 OUNCE **ESPRESSO**, HOT OR AT ROOM TEMPERATURE

BLOOD ORANGE JUICE AIR (SEE BELOW), FOR GARNISH

\\\\\\

In a shaker with ice, combine the Cynar, cassis, and espresso. Shake hard, then strain into a glass of your choice. Garnish with a stain of blood orange juice air.

BLOOD ORANGE JUICE AIR

MAKES 10 SERVINGS

1 CUP FRESH **BLOOD ORANGE JUICE**

1 TEASPOON **TEXTURAS SUCRO**
(SUCROSE ESTERS; SEE SOURCES, PAGE 153)

Combine the blood orange juice and Sucro in a bowl and zap it with an immersion blender. A light, bubbly foam will form; it should hold for 10 to 15 minutes. Continue to zap it as needed to refresh.

Nocino is a liqueur made from young—or "green"—black walnuts. Its preparation is celebrated every year in Italy in June. I exclude cloves and allspice from this recipe because I like the nocino to be served at all times of the year, and often cloves and allspice are synonymous with Thanksgiving and Christmas.

The walnuts will stain your hands black, so you might want to wear latex gloves when handling them. • **MAKES 30 (1-OUNCE) SERVINGS**

NOCINO

〰〰

25 UNRIPE **(GREEN) BLACK WALNUTS**, CUT IN HALF

8 **WILD BAY LEAVES**

2 **VANILLA BEANS**, SPLIT LENGTHWISE

8 **BLACK MISSION FIGS**, CUT IN HALF

4 **CINNAMON STICKS**

SPRIG OF **WHITE FIR OR FRESH PINE** (FROM A PINE TREE)

2 (750-ML) BOTTLES **BOYD & BLAIR 151 POTATO VODKA**

ABOUT 3½ CUPS **HONEY SYRUP** (SEE PAGE 144)

〰〰

Place the walnuts, bay leaves, vanilla beans, figs, cinnamon sticks, and fir sprig in a 3-quart jar. Fill the

(recipe continues)

jar to the top with the vodka, cover, and set aside in a cool, dark place to infuse for 4 months. Every week or two, agitate the jar by stirring the infusion with a long spoon or tipping the sealed jar upside down a few times. After 4 months, strain the mixture into a clean 3-quart jar.

Add the honey syrup to the unsweetened nocino and stir well. It is very important that the honey syrup you add to the strained infusion equals one-half of the volume. For example, if you end up with 8 cups unsweetened nocino, you add 4 cups honey syrup. Cover the nocino and set it aside in a cool, dark place for 1 month before using. It will keep for up to 1 year or longer.

CapRock bitter is a wine-based amaro that is so delicious on its own that I don't need to drink anything else in the world ever again. It is part of the Peak Spirits portfolio and happens to be one of the only biodynamic spirits created in North America.

Bronze fennel is a darker and sweeter version of regular fennel; it is the perfect thing to chew on after a large meal. • **MAKES 1**

WHITE BALSAMIC NEGRONI

1 OUNCE **CAPROCK GIN**

1 OUNCE **DOLIN BLANC**

1 OUNCE **CAPROCK BITTER**

¼ OUNCE **WHITE RASPBERRY BALSAMIC VINEGAR**
(SEE SOURCES, PAGE 153)

SPRIG OF **HUACATAY**, FOR GARNISH

PICKLED MUSTARD SEEDS, FOR GARNISH (OPTIONAL)

BRONZE FENNEL FRONDS OR OTHER **AROMATIC HERB LEAVES**, FOR GARNISH (OPTIONAL)

(recipe continues)

Pour the gin, Dolin, bitter, and vinegar into a mixing glass with ice and stir until frost appears on the glass. Strain into a coupe or several shot glasses and garnish with the sprig of huacatay (alternatively, drop some pickled mustard seeds to the bottom of the glass and garnish with bronze fennel fronds).

This is a very rich, juicy, and citrus-forward version of the Negroni. • **MAKES 1**

NEVER LET ME GO

//////

2 OUNCES **CYNAR**

½ OUNCE **CRÈME DE CASSIS**

2 OUNCES FRESH **BLOOD ORANGE JUICE**

SUNFLOWER PETALS, FOR GARNISH

BLOOD ORANGE CRACKER (SEE PAGE 9), FOR GARNISH

//////

In a cocktail shaker with ice, combine the Cynar, crème de cassis, and blood orange juice. Shake, then strain into a rocks glass filled with ice and garnish with the sunflower petals and a blood orange cracker.

Sweet clover grows around the mountains of Los Angeles in the spring. It belongs to the alfalfa family and has nuances of tarragon, clove, and the forest that sit well in the Cocchi Americano. • **MAKES 1**

SWEET CLOVER MARTINI

3 OUNCES **MONKEY 47 GIN**

1 OUNCE **SWEET CLOVER–INFUSED COCCHI AMERICANO ROSA** (SEE OPPOSITE)

4 DASHES OF **FENNEL BITTERS**

SPRIG OF **WILD ELDERFLOWER**, FOR GARNISH

In a mixing glass with ice, combine the gin, infused Cocchi Americano Rosa, and fennel bitters, then strain into a coupe and garnish with the wild elderflower sprig.

SWEET CLOVER-INFUSED COCCHI AMERICANO ROSA

MAKES 1 (750-ML) BOTTLE

2 HANDFULS OF **SWEET CLOVER**

1 (750-ML) BOTTLE **COCCHI AMERICANO ROSA**

Place the clover in a quart-size jar and pour in the Cocchi
Americano Rosa. Cover and refrigerate for 1 week.
Strain back into the bottle. The infusion will keep in the
refrigerator for up to 2 months.

The glass I use for this drink, a Quaffer (see Sources, page 153), was originally designed for Jäger bombs. Once I saw it, I knew that I had greater aspirations for it and thought it would be amazing to use to serve a layered drink that had two distinct flavors. The best part about this is using a Luxardo cherry that has been soaked in kirsch to block the hole between the two layers. • **MAKES 1**

THE ANTIDOTE

\\\\\

BOTTOM LAYER
2 OUNCES **BURDOCK-INFUSED BOURBON**
(RECIPE FOLLOWS)

¼ OUNCE **AGAVE SYRUP** (SEE PAGE 32)

5 DASHES OF **ANGOSTURA BITTERS**

1 **LUXARDO MARASCHINO CHERRY**

TOP LAYER
2 OUNCES **STINGING NETTLE–INFUSED GIN**
(RECIPE FOLLOWS)

½ OUNCE **YELLOW CHARTREUSE**

½ OUNCE FRESH **RUBY RED GRAPEFRUIT JUICE**

½ OUNCE FRESH **LEMON JUICE**

¼ OUNCE **AGAVE SYRUP**

\\\\\

(recipe continues)

Pour the infused bourbon, agave, and bitters into a mixing glass with ice and stir until there is frost on the glass. Pour into the bottom section of a Quaffer. Then take the Luxardo cherry and block the hole.

In a cocktail shaker with ice, combine the infused gin, chartreuse, grapefruit juice, lemon juice, and agave. Shake, then strain into the top section of the Quaffer.

BURDOCK-INFUSED BOURBON

MAKES 1 (750-ML) BOTTLE

½ POUND FRESH **BURDOCK ROOT**

1 (750-ML) BOTTLE **ELIJAH CRAIG 12-YEAR BOURBON**

Place the burdock root in a 2-quart jar and pour in the bourbon. Cover and set aside in a cool, dark place to infuse for 1 week. Strain the bourbon back into the bottle. It will keep in the refrigerator for up to 3 months.

STINGING NETTLE-INFUSED GIN

MAKES 1 (750-ML) BOTTLE

½ POUND FRESH **STINGING NETTLES**

1 (750-ML) BOTTLE **CAPROCK GIN**

Wearing gloves or using tongs, place the nettles in a
2-quart jar and pour in the gin. Cover and set aside in a
cool, dark place to infuse for 1 week. Strain the gin back
into the bottle. It will keep in the refrigerator for up to
3 months.

The longer calvados is aged, the smoother it becomes. The apple cider flavor is so prominent that it seemed to be a perfect drink to serve warm.

WARM TEA

////

2 OUNCES **CALVADOS**

¾ OUNCE **HONEY SYRUP** (SEE BELOW)

¾ FRESH **LEMON JUICE**

2 OUNCES HOT **EARL GREY TEA** (SEE OPPOSITE)

////

Pour the calvados, honey syrup, lemon juice, and tea into a teacup, stir together, and serve.

HONEY SYRUP

MAKES 4 CUPS

In a small saucepan, bring 1 cup water to a boil. Pour in 3 cups **honey** (preferably buckwheat honey). Stir until all the honey has dissolved. Let cool, then strain the syrup into a glass bottle and seal. The syrup will keep in the refrigerator for up to 1 month.

EARL GREY TEA

MAKES 1 CUP

Pour 2 ounces loose **Earl Grey tea** in the filter of a glass teapot and pour 1 cup of boiling water over it. Let it sit for 2 minutes, then remove the tea and filter.

This is my triple-infused spirited cocktail: it has three of my favorite spirits infused with three of my favorite things. The cacao rum by SelvaRey is one of the most flavorful and perfected infused spirits on the market. It is made in Panama by Master Distiller Don Pancho and has been aged in bourbon barrels for five years. • **MAKES 1**

WILD CACAO RUM

\\\\\\

1 OUNCE **WILD BAY–INFUSED CACAO RUM**
(RECIPE FOLLOWS)

1 OUNCE **STRAWBERRY-INFUSED CHAREAU**
(RECIPE FOLLOWS)

1 OUNCE **MUSHROOM-INFUSED CYNAR**
(RECIPE FOLLOWS)

GRAPEFRUIT TWIST, FOR GARNISH

2 SPRIGS OF **WILD BAY LEAVES**, FOR GARNISH

\\\\\\

Pour the rum, Chareau, and Cynar into a mixing glass with ice and stir until frost appears on the glass. Strain into a rocks glass with ice and garnish with a grapefruit twist and the wild bay leaves.

WILD BAY-INFUSED CACAO RUM

MAKES 1 (750-ML) BOTTLE

8 TO 10 **WILD OR REGULAR BAY LEAVES**

1 (750-ML) BOTTLE **SELVAREY CACAO RUM**

Split the bay leaves in half, place them in a quart-size jar, and pour in the rum. Cover and set aside in a cool, dark place to infuse for 1 week. Strain the rum back into the bottle. It will keep in a cool, dark place for up to 3 months.

STRAWBERRY-INFUSED CHAREAU

MAKES 1 (750-ML) BOTTLE

2 PINTS FRESH **STRAWBERRIES**, HULLED AND HALVED

1 (750-ML) BOTTLE **CHAREAU ALOE VERA LIQUEUR**

Place the strawberries in a 2-quart jar and pour in the Chareau. Cover and let sit in a cool, dark place to infuse for 1 week. Strain the Chareau back into the bottle. It will keep in the refrigerator for up to 3 months.

MUSHROOM-INFUSED CYNAR

MAKES 1 (1-L) BOTTLE

1 OUNCE DRIED **CANDY CAP MUSHROOMS**

1 (1-L) BOTTLE **CYNAR**

Place the mushrooms in a quart-size jar and pour in the Cynar. Cover and let sit in a cool, dark place to infuse for 1 week. Strain the Cynar back into the bottle. It will keep in a cool, dark place for up to 6 months.

UNIVERSAL CONVERSION CHART

OVEN TEMPERATURE EQUIVALENTS

250°F = 120°C

275°F = 135°C

300°F = 150°C

325°F = 160°C

350°F = 180°C

375°F = 190°C

400°F = 200°C

425°F = 220°C

450°F = 230°C

475°F = 240°C

500°F = 260°C

MEASUREMENT EQUIVALENTS

Measurements should always be level unless directed otherwise.

⅛ TEASPOON = 0.5 ML

¼ TEASPOON = 1 ML

½ TEASPOON = 2 ML

1 TEASPOON = 5 ML

1 TABLESPOON = 3 TEASPOONS = ½ FLUID OUNCE = 15 ML

2 TABLESPOONS = ⅛ CUP = 1 FLUID OUNCE = 30 ML

4 TABLESPOONS = ¼ CUP = 2 FLUID OUNCES = 60 ML

5⅓ TABLESPOONS = ⅓ CUP = 3 FLUID OUNCES = 80 ML

8 TABLESPOONS = ½ CUP = 4 FLUID OUNCES = 120 ML

10⅔ TABLESPOONS = ⅔ CUP = 5 FLUID OUNCES = 160 ML

12 TABLESPOONS = ¾ CUP = 6 FLUID OUNCES = 180 ML

16 TABLESPOONS = 1 CUP = 8 FLUID OUNCES = 240 ML

SOURCES

//////

AMEDEI: Chocolate products, including hot chocolate powder
amedei.it

BONJOUR: Specialty kitchen tools and small appliances, including kitchen torches
bonjourproducts.com

BUBBIES: Horseradish and other prepared foods
bubbies.com

CLOVER: Fresh juice products
cloverjuice.com

HEPP'S SALT CO.: Specialty salts, including applewood smoked salt, ghost pepper sea salt, and Himalayan pink salt slabs
heppssalt.com

ISI CULINARY: Cream whippers and N_2O chargers
isi.com/us

MODERNIST PANTRY: Modernist cuisine ingredients and supplies, including Texturas Sucro (sucrose esters) and Superbags
modernistpantry.com

NESCO: Food dehydrators and other small kitchen appliances
nesco.com

NUVO OLIVE OIL: Organic olive oils and infused vinegars, including white raspberry balsamic vinegar
nuvooliveoil.com

POLYSCIENCE: The Smoking Gun and wood chips for smoking
http://polyscienceculinary.com

QUAFFER: Specialty shot glasses
quaffer.com

VANILLA FROM TAHITI: Vanilla beans and other vanilla products
vanillafromtahiti.com

VITAMIX: High-speed blenders
vitamix.com

LIQUORS

123 TEQUILA: Organic 100% agave tequilas in three ages: Blanco (Uno), Reposado (Dos), and Añejo (Tres)
123tequila.com

BASIL HAYDEN'S: Kentucky straight bourbon whiskey
basilhaydens.com

BÉNÉDICTINE: Herbal liqueur
http://benedictinedom.com

BENESIN TOBALA: Organic mezcal
benesin.com

BOYD & BLAIR: 80 proof and 151 proof potato vodkas
boydandblair.com

CALISAYA: Liqueur derived from cinchona bark
calisaya.net

CAPPELLETTI VINO APERITIVO AMERICANO ROSSO:
Vermouth-based bitter
cappellettinovasalus.it/eng

CAPURRO: Pisco, in four varietals
http://piscocapurro.com

CAPROCK: Colorado-made gin, vodka, and brandies
http://peakspirits.com/caprock

CHAREAU: California-made aloe vera liqueur
http://chareau.us

COCCHI: Sparkling and aromatized wines, including
Americano Rosa, and spirits
cocchi.it/eng

COGNAC PARK: Single-vineyard cognac
cognac-park.com/en

CYNAR: Artichoke-based liqueur
camparigroup.com/en/brands/liqueursothers/cynar

DOLIN: Vermouths and various liqueurs
dolin.fr/gb

ELIJAH CRAIG: 12-year-old Kentucky straight bourbon
*bardstownwhiskeysociety.com/brands/elijah-craig-single-
barrel.php*

FORDS GIN: London-distilled gin
fordsgin.com

GENEVIEVE: Genever-style (distilled dry) gin
anchordistilling.com/brand/anchor/#genevieve-gin

GRAND MARNIER: Orange-flavored cognac-based liqueur
http://grand-marnier.com

HEERING CHERRY LIQUEUR: Cherry brandy
heering.com

HENDRICK'S GIN: Gin infused with rose and cucumber
us.hendricksgin.com

HOPHEAD: Vodka distilled with hops
anchordistilling.com/brand/anchor/#hophead-vodka

KROGSTAD: Oregon-made aquavit in two styles: Festlig
(unaged) and Gamle (aged for 12 months in oak wine
barrels)
http://housespirits.com/spirits

LAPHROAIG: Islay single-malt Scotch whiskies
laphroaig.com

MONKEY 47: Schwarzwald dry gin distilled from
47 ingredients
monkey47.com

NOVO FOGO: Cachaça in a variety of styles and ages
novofogo.com

PIMM'S: Gin-based fruit liqueur
anyoneforpimms.com

PUNT E MES: Vermouth with added bitters
carpano.com/en/products/punt-e-mes

SELVAREY: Panama white and cacao rums
selvarey.com

ST. ELIZABETH ALLSPICE DRAM: Allspice-flavored liqueur

ST-GERMAIN: Elderflower liqueur
st-germain.fr

INDEX

////